Clemons Van Forer's Freedom
The Escape

Joshua Augustus Clemons

McPubKids

A Division of McClure Publishing, Inc.

Joshua Augustus Clemons Copyright © 2024 by McPubKids, a division of McClure Publishing, Inc.
1st Edition—ISBN 979-8-9877802-7-5

Published in the United States by McClure Publishing, Inc. | Bloomingdale, Illinois | 800.659.4908

https://www.McPubKids.com
books@McPubKids.com

Illustrator: Lamont Wayne

Editor: Jennifer Lipford Petticolas
jlp7139@yahoo.com

Filed under Library of Congress Catalog Number: 2024905010

I dedicate this book to my ancestors, especially to my GG, Clytie Rosser Lipford.

"I am done!" said John. He looked up from the computer screen. It had taken him a long time, but he had finally finished. He was proud of what he accomplished.

His mother called out asking, "John, what are you doing?"

"I just finished writing another story about Clemons Van Forer!" said John. "Do you want to hear it?"

"Yes! I would love to!" said his mother. "I'm coming."

It was a sweltering summer day. The heat was rising like fire from under the earth. It felt like the sun was throwing hot coals down to the earth which disintegrated sinking below the surface of the ground. Sweat was dripping, and Clemons's muscles were tired. He felt he could not pick another piece of cotton.

Clemons looked across the field at his sons. He knew his sons were feeling the exact same pain he was feeling.

Clemons's sons Rob and Larry were tall, slender, and muscular like their father. Rob was now fifteen years old, and Larry was eleven years old.

Meanwhile in the house, Clemons's daughter, Mateia, now fourteen years old was cleaning dust from the top of wardrobe in the master bedroom. She could hear the master and the overseer talking.

"There is an auction in town on Tuesday," said the owner. "I was thinking if we could sell those old Clemons boys."

The overseer asked, "Do you think they will bring enough to save the plantation?"

"I'm not sure," said the owner. "If they don't bring much money, just keep them."

Mateia froze. She could not believe what she had heard! She had to go tell her mother right away! But she waited for them to leave. When she thought they were gone, she eased her way down from the stool. Her legs were trembling from fear like leaves swaying on a tree.

She walked down the hallway, taking big steps so the wooden floor would not creak. As she walked down the hall, she saw the overseer and the owner in the library. She was sure the overseer and the owner would catch her, but they were too busy talking to notice her.

When Mateia entered the kitchen she saw Shaka, her mother, wiping sweat from her forehead with her apron while stirring a pot of stew.

When Shaka saw her daughter, she smiled. She gave her daughter a hug and kissed her on the top of her head. Mateia looked around to make sure they were alone. Then she whispered in her mother's ear. Shaka stared at Mateia. Then she said, "We'll talk about this in the cabin. Go back to doing your cleaning."

At the end of the day, they all assembled outside the cabin. Shaka told the family that Rob and Larry were going to be sold. Clemons looked skyward.

The sky looked like it was angry, with a mind that was about to explode! Clemons uttered, "God, guide us."

Clemons and Shaka watched their children as they slept. They were worried about what would happen to their family if they were caught while trying to escape.

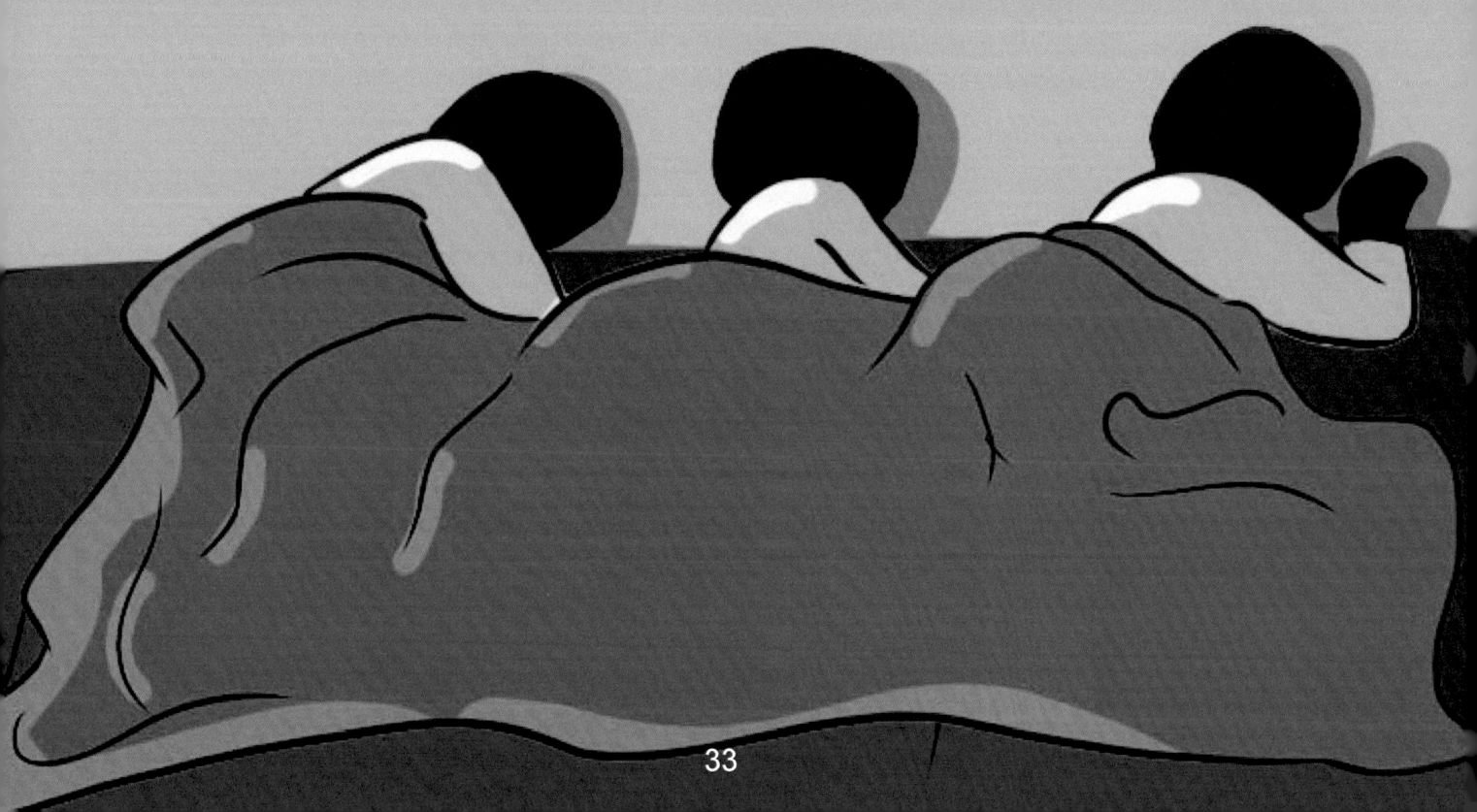

At midnight, they woke the children. They were all full of nervous energy. They were ready to escape from the waking nightmare that their ancestors had lived since slave hunters captured and forced them on new soil.

The Forer family snuck out of their cabin and ran into the woods. After running for a long while, they stopped and sat on a giant log. They rested a short while and started again.

They stumbled over stumps and through thick brushes. Larry could feel pain as his leg scrapped against a stump. They kept running and running. Faster and faster. Soon enough, their legs started aching.

Mateia's dress got stuck on a thorn. The thorn pierced through to her skin. She started bleeding badly. Tears ran down Mateia's cheeks.

They stopped in a small clearing. The forest was dark, but the slivered moon was shining. The only sounds were owls hooting and crickets chirping. Clemons ripped off the bottom of his shirt to wrap Mateia's wound.

Looking at his daughter, Clemons said, "It's still dark and no one has missed us yet. I think we should turn back."

Suddenly a soft gruffy voice whispered, "Don't turn back."

"Who said that?" asked Clemons.

An old man appeared covered in mud. He seemed to have stepped out of the trunk of the tree.

Clemons stepped in front of his family. "Who are you?" Clemons asked.

"My name is Steplight."

"Can you help us? My daughter is bleeding and scared," said Clemons.

The old man peeked over at Mateia. "I can stop the bleeding."

Shaka packed mud and moss, Steplight had gathered, in her daughter's side. The bleeding stopped.

"It is going to be light soon. If you are not turning back, I can take you to a place where you will be safe and can get some rest, but we will need to go now."

Clemons looked at his family. Rob said, "Daddy, we don't want to go back. Larry nodded in agreement.

Clemons turned to Steplight and said, "Lead the way."

The forest was dark; it was nearing the end of the moon phase. A waxing crescent was in the sky. The crescent was as skinny as a starving stray dog.

Larry asked, "How can he know what is the right way? Everything looks alike."

"A trick the elders shared on the plantation was to follow the moss on the trees, follow the Drinking Gourd, and most important, follow the North Star," said Clemons. "Heaven sees the North Star every night, and heaven knows we are escaping."

"Amen," said Shaka.

Light was slowly creeping across the sky. When they came to a huge foggy marshy area, Steplight, said, "We will stop here to rest for a short while."

The Forer family shared their yams with Steplight.

After they ate, they followed Steplight into the fog. They trudged through mud and tall grass.

"Stay close," said Steplight. "Walk in my footsteps. There are spots that will suck you in."

Larry said, "My legs feel like they're swaying against the water in the pond, on the plantation in winter." He shivered, and his teeth chattered.

"Just keep walking," said Steplight.

Suddenly through the fog, an island appeared.

"What is this?" Shaka asked.

"This is where I live!" Steplight exclaimed.

Two guards were guarding the entrance which was on the south side of the settlement. There were guards in treetops and five guards on the north side. Cypress trees surrounded the settlement.

"We have guards on the look-out in case any bears, bobcats, or unwanted guests arrive," Steplight said.

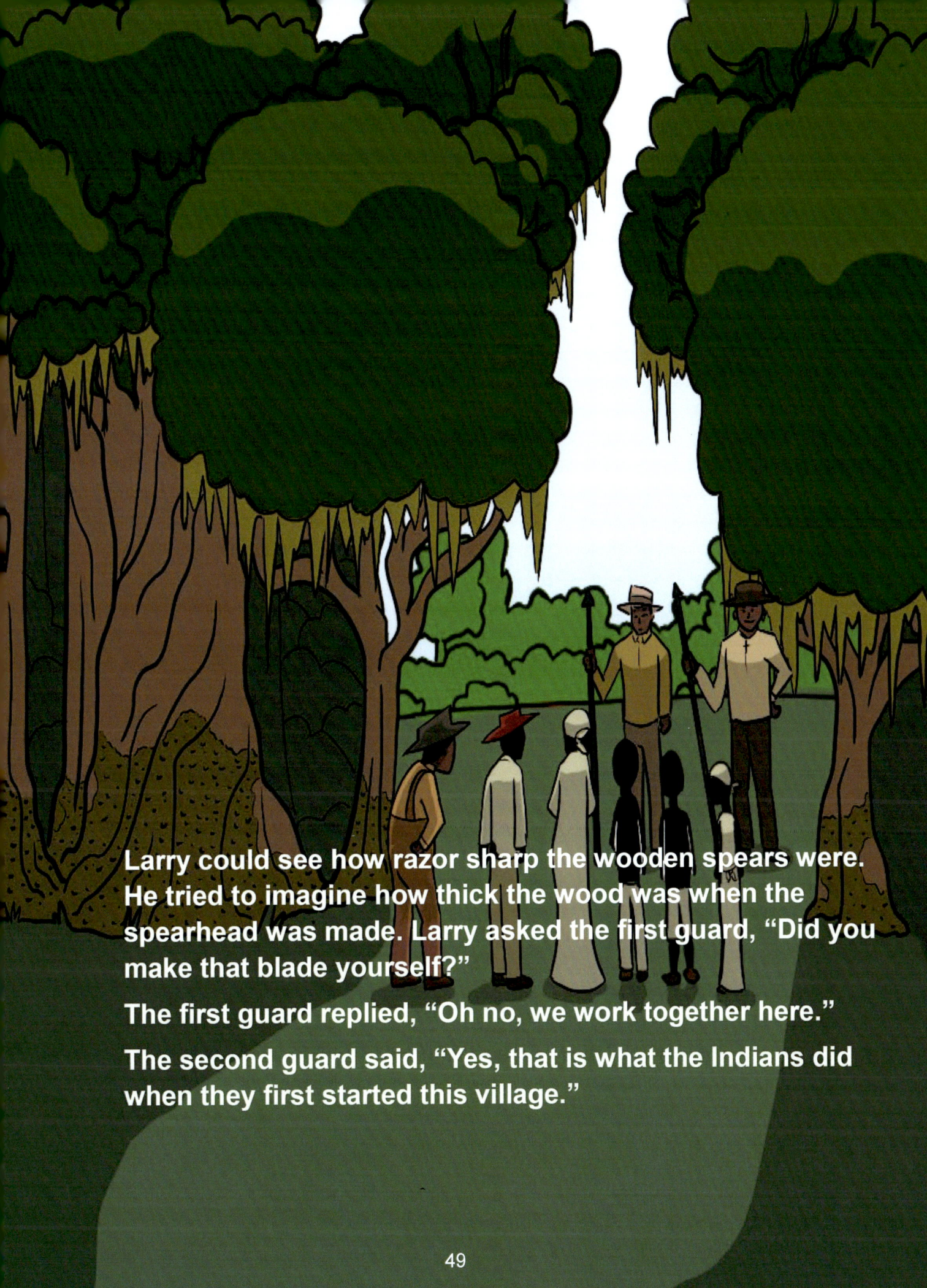

Larry could see how razor sharp the wooden spears were. He tried to imagine how thick the wood was when the spearhead was made. Larry asked the first guard, "Did you make that blade yourself?"

The first guard replied, "Oh no, we work together here."

The second guard said, "Yes, that is what the Indians did when they first started this village."

John's mother interrupted his reading. "Wait, how do you know about the enslaved living in swampy areas?"

"I read *Freewater* by Amina Luqman-Dawson," said John. "Not all escaped enslaved people went north. Some of them stayed in swampy areas near the plantations where their families were. I wanted to show that in the Great Dismal Swamp area, Maroons survived and ran their own villages just like in Africa!"

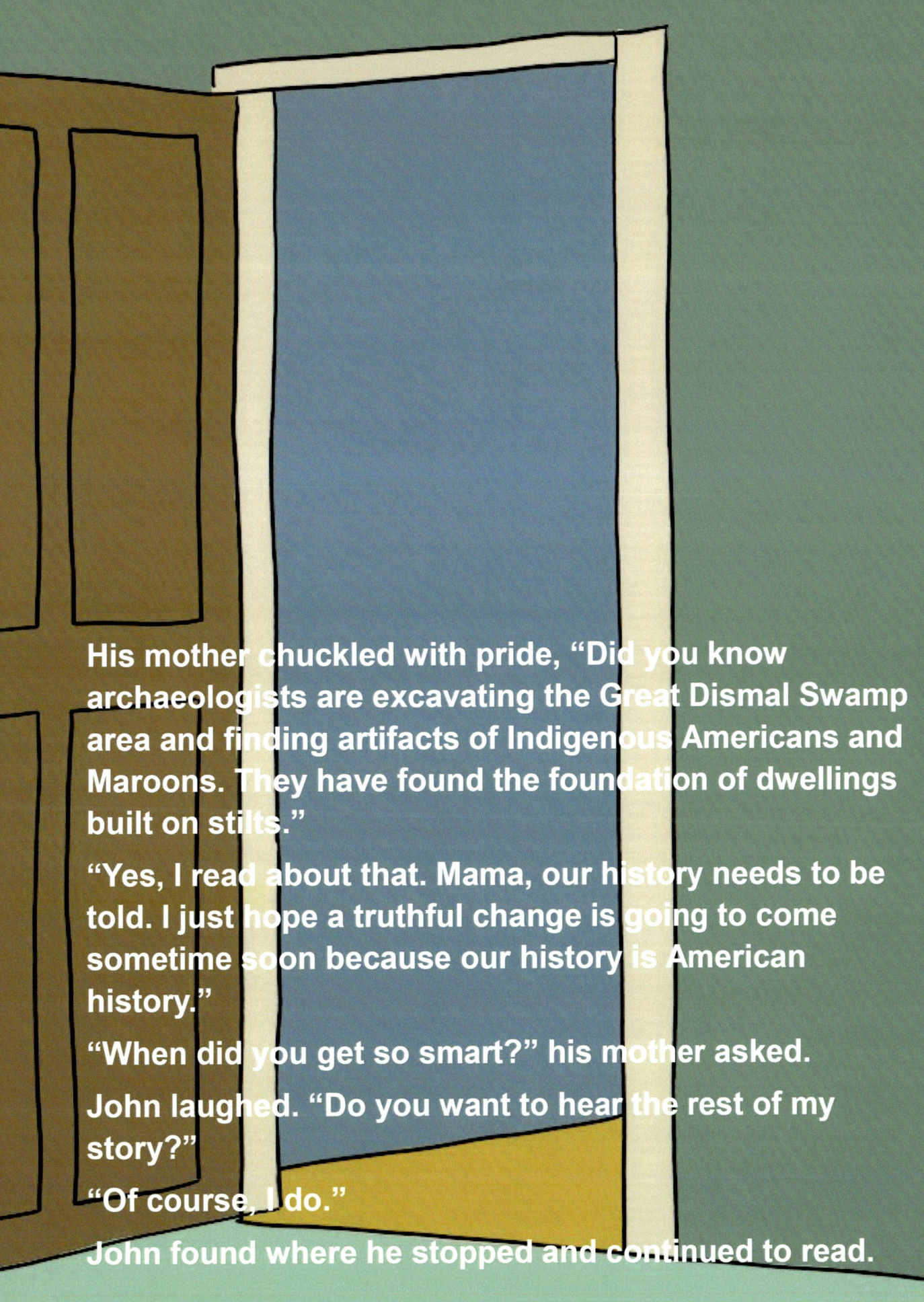

His mother chuckled with pride, "Did you know archaeologists are excavating the Great Dismal Swamp area and finding artifacts of Indigenous Americans and Maroons. They have found the foundation of dwellings built on stilts."

"Yes, I read about that. Mama, our history needs to be told. I just hope a truthful change is going to come sometime soon because our history is American history."

"When did you get so smart?" his mother asked.

John laughed. "Do you want to hear the rest of my story?"

"Of course, I do."

John found where he stopped and continued to read.

Rob noticed the cypress trees lined up like soldiers. There were beautiful flowers. The grass was as green as emerald, and the birds were chirping in harmony that sounded like the old Negro spiritual - steal away … steal away home.

There were children sitting around an elderly woman sitting on an old tree stump. Rob turned to Steplight and asked, "Who is that elderly woman?"

Steplight smiled and said, "Her name is Clytie. She is a woman of wisdom and the keeper of all our stories. She tells our stories, to the children, of our villages in Africa when we were kings and queens."

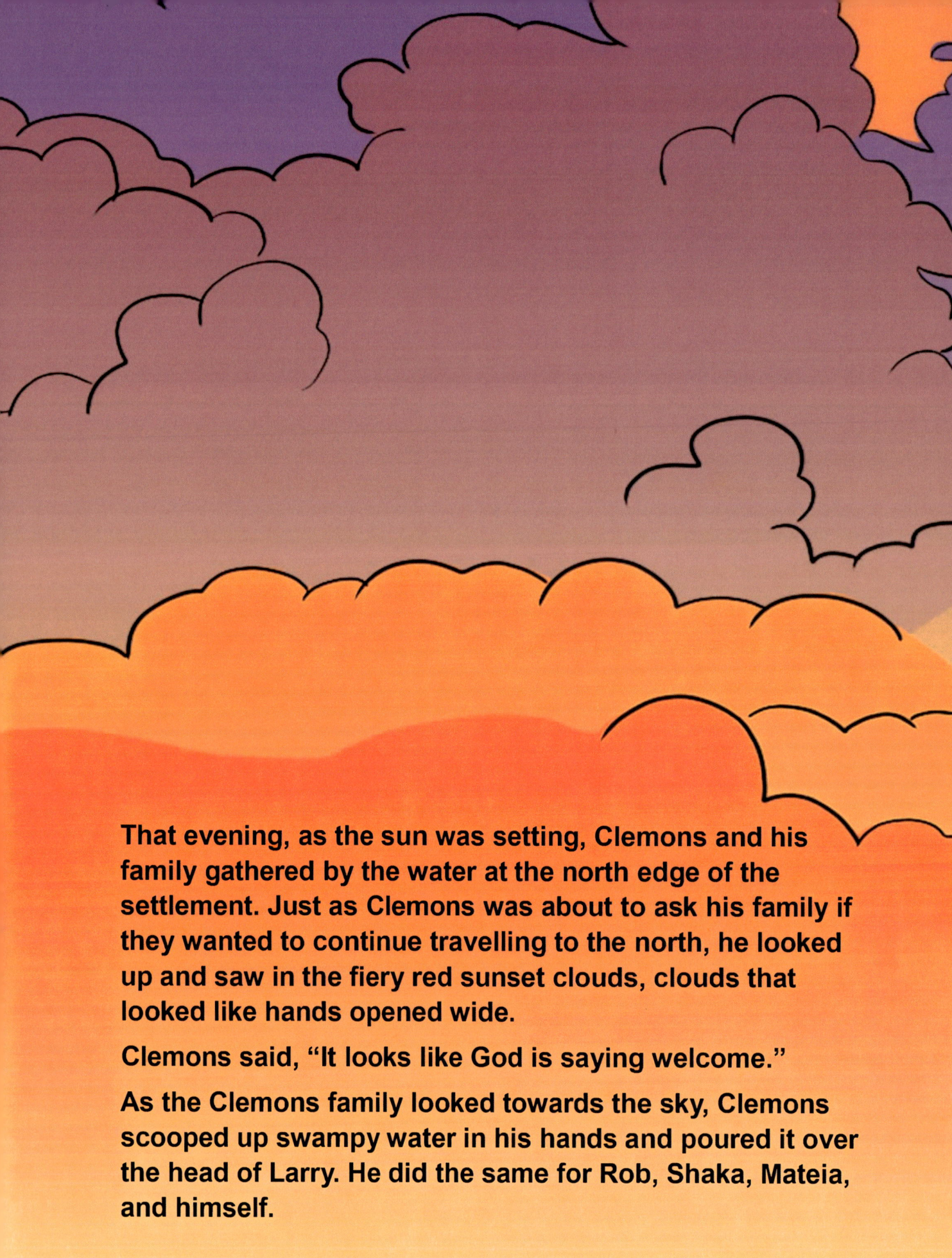

That evening, as the sun was setting, Clemons and his family gathered by the water at the north edge of the settlement. Just as Clemons was about to ask his family if they wanted to continue travelling to the north, he looked up and saw in the fiery red sunset clouds, clouds that looked like hands opened wide.

Clemons said, "It looks like God is saying welcome."

As the Clemons family looked towards the sky, Clemons scooped up swampy water in his hands and poured it over the head of Larry. He did the same for Rob, Shaka, Mateia, and himself.

Clemons and his family fell on their knees. Clemons said, "Praise God for our new home."

"The End!" John said.

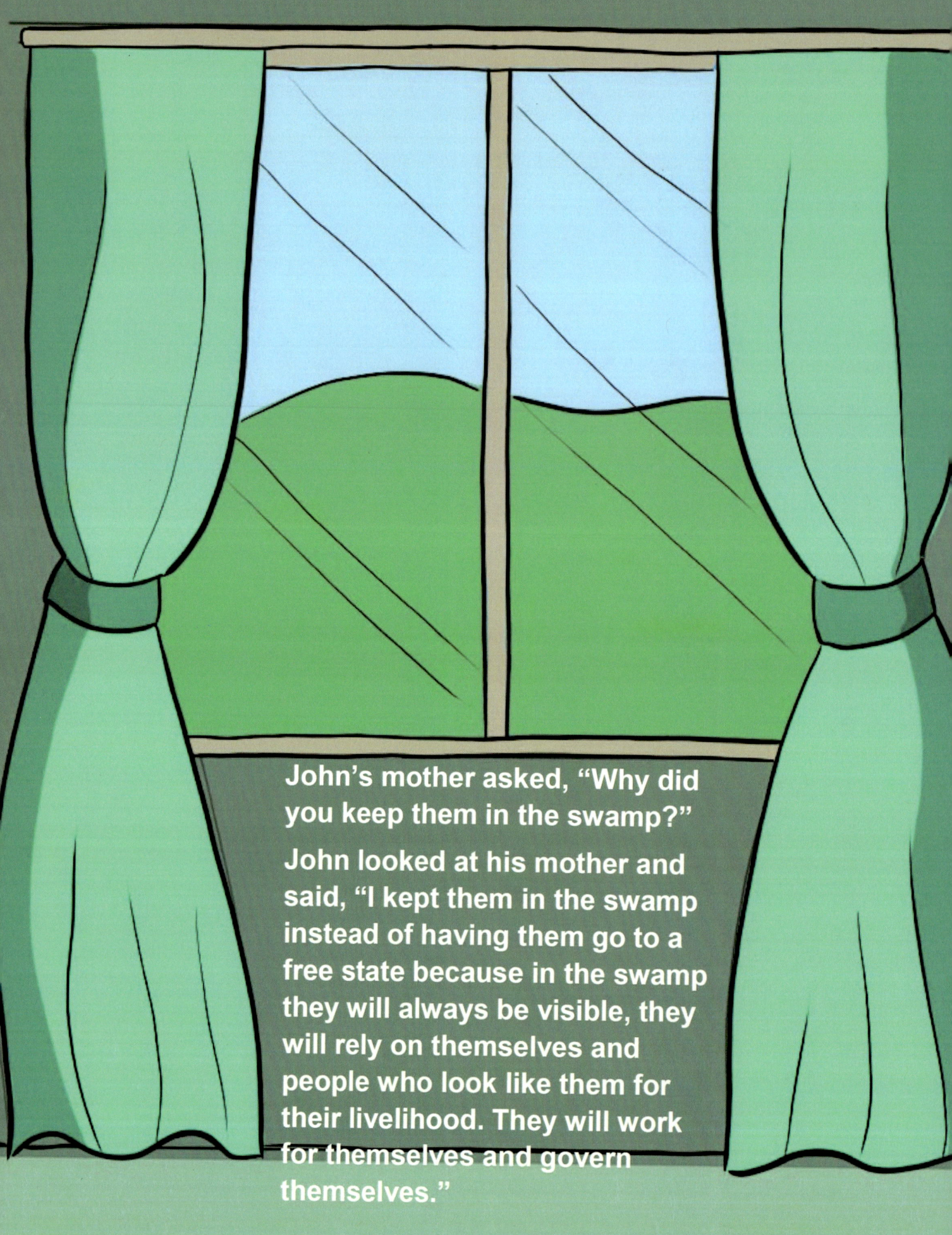

" Wow, I'm stunned!" his mother said. "You are a very good writer!"

"You think so?" John asked.

"I know so," his mother said with a jolt of happiness.

"Maybe I could draft a story about forgiveness!" John said.

"Well, the world is a magical place," his mother said.

"It sure is," John said. "It sure is!"

Glossary

Archaeologist: a person who studies history by excavating different sites to find artifacts.

Great Dismal Swamp: the large swamp in the coastal plain region of Southeastern Virginia and North Carolina.

Excavating: a careful removal of earth to find buried history.

Indigenous Americans: people who lived in America before the Europeans.

Maroons: enslaved people who escaped and formed their own communities in the Great Dismal Swamp.

Overseer: a person who was over the enslaved on a plantation.

Plantation: a large farm with crops like cotton and tobacco worked by enslaved people.

Steal Away: is an old Negro Spiritual which was composed by Wallace Willis, an enslaved man.

The Drinking Gourd: is the constellation known as the Big Dipper. The pointer stars at the end of the Big Dipper always point to the North Star. As the earth rotates all stars move around the North Star. The North Star stays pointing North and the Drinking Gourd is always near the North Star.

Yam: a starchy tuber (underground part of the potato). Yams are native to Africa, Asia, and the Caribbean.

The Great Dismal Swamp

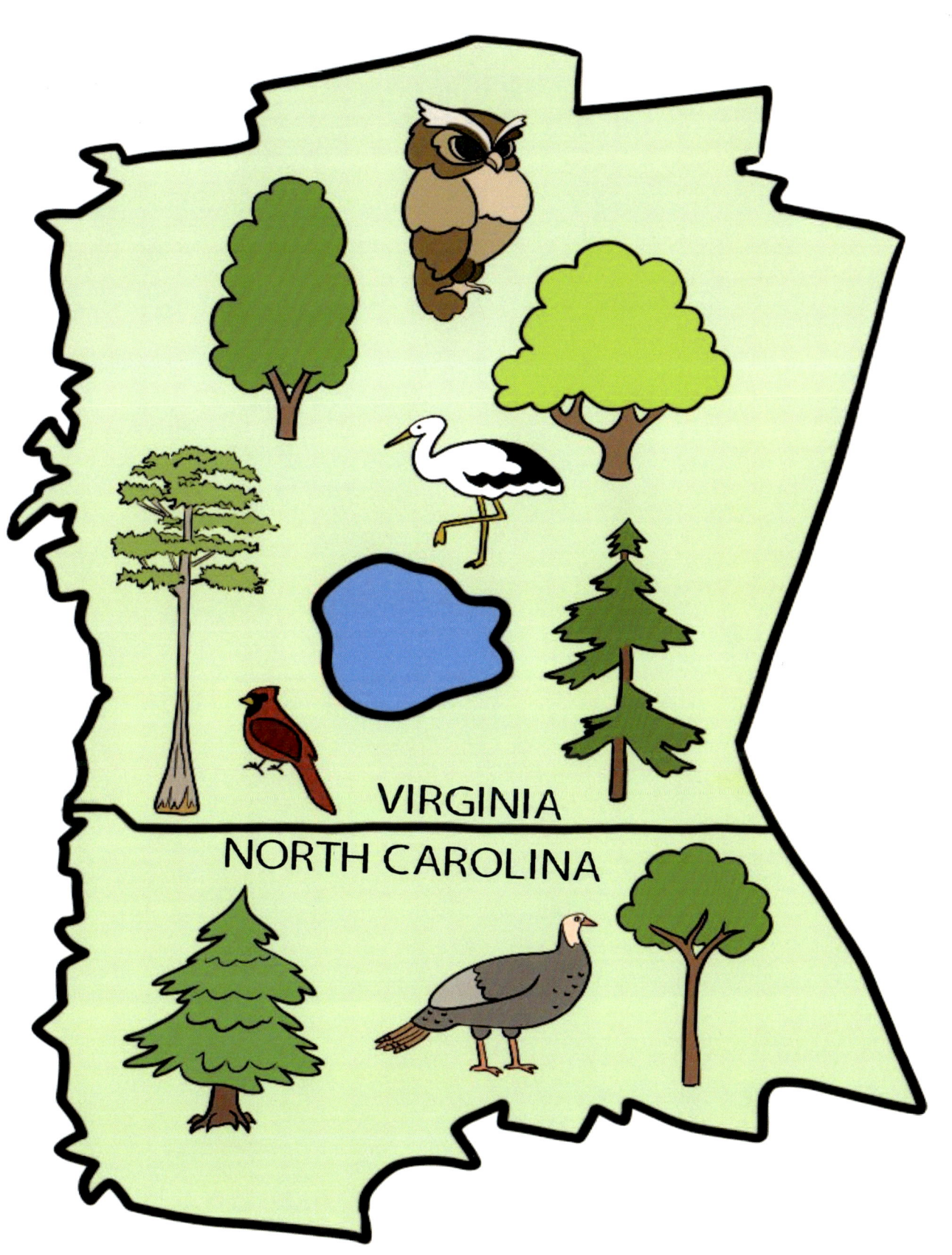

The Great Dismal Swamp

View the pictures above. Can you explain how this area possibly got the name Great Dismal Swamp?

Bald Cypress Tree

The Bald Cypress Tree, a conifer tree, is a slow growing tree that can live for hundreds of years. Many conifers are evergreens. Bald Cypress Trees are deciduous. They shed their leaves in the fall of the year; they appear bald.

Knees of the Bald Cypress Tree.

A special feature of the Bald Cypress Tree is its knees, which bring oxygen to the roots of the tree.

Lake Drummond

Lake Drummond is the highest point in the Great Dismal Swamp. It is one of two freshwater lakes in Virginia. No one is sure how the lake was formed.

There are three possible theories: (1) A meteorite created the depression for the lake. (2) A Native American legend says the lake was formed when a great "firebird" built a fiery nest in the center of the swamp. (3) A wildfire burned peat soil down to sand forming the depression for the lake.

Creative writing activity: Write a paragraph. Make up your own theory of how Lake Drummond was formed.

Study Questions

1. What is history?
2. Is history important? Why?
3. Who is the keeper of history in this story?
4. What is a plantation?
5. In what state is the plantation where the Forer family is enslaved? Explain your answer.
6. What is an overseer?
7. Why did Clemons and his family escape from the plantation?
8. What did Clemons and his family pack to plant when they reached freedom?
9. What is geography?
10. Describe the geography of the plantation.
11. Describe the geography of the Great Dismal Swamp.
12. How does geography affect the environment and the way people live?
13. Who is Steplight? Why do you think his name is Steplight?
14. Who first lived in the swamp village?
15. Why was the house, in the swamp, raised from the ground?
16. What type of tree is mentioned in the story?
17. Who were the Maroons?
18. Did Maroons feel safe living in the swamp? Why or why not?
19. What did Clemons see that made him decide that the swamp was their new home?
20. How are people now learning about the Great Dismal Swamp communities?
21. Who are our ancestors?
22. Why do you think Clemons poured water over the heads of his family?
23. Why did John keep Clemons and his family in the swamp?
24. Why do you think Clemons and his family do not have faces until the end of the story?
25. What is freedom?

Suggested Reading

Freewater by Amina Luqman-Dawson

About the Author

Joshua Augustus Clemons is ten years old. He is in the fifth grade. He published his first book, *Clemons Van Forer's Freedom*, when he was eight years old. Joshua enjoys writing and creating fictional stories. Not only does he love writing, but Joshua also loves playing tennis, soccer, and chess. He enjoys drawing, singing, and dancing. What he loves most is spending time with his family, friends, and his dogs, Josie and Nugget. Joshua strongly believes in prayer. He loves talking to God.

www.ingramcontent.com/pod-product-compliance
Lightning Source LLC
LaVergne TN
LVRC090726070526
838199LV00019B/546